#ActuallyICan

The Art of Affirming Yourself to Greatness

KELSEY AIDA ROUALDES

DISCLAIMER:

This book is not about feeling good all the time. If you felt good all the time you would actually be numb and feel nothing. **#NOTHANKS**

This book is about honoring all feelings and then choosing to feel better when the time is right for you.

This book is about releasing resistance to life and feeling better more of the time.

This book is about feeling good on purpose and choosing happiness for yourself.

This book is about you stepping into your power.

Honor yourself, honor how you feel, and most importantly have fun affirming yourself to greatness.

SIDE
EFFECTS:

SIDE EFFECTS OF READING #ACTUALLYICAN MAY INCLUDE, BUT ARE NOT LIMITED TO...

INCREASED LEVELS OF SELF CONFIDENCE

LOTS OF MONEY

UNEXPLAINABLE EXCITEMENT ABOUT LIFE

INNER PEACE

UNBELIEVABLE HEALTH

ALL AROUND BADASSERY

AND OF COURSE DEATH, OF YOUR EGO.

PART 1: EVERYTHING YOU COULD EVER NEED TO KNOW ABOUT HOW TO GET POSITIVE AFFIRMATIONS TO ACTUALLY WORK FOR YOU

"MONEY FLOWS INTO MY LIFE EASILY AND EFFORTLESSLY."

Try telling that to my bank account..

"I LOVE MYSELF AND EMBRACE ALL MY FLAWS."

... more like erase all my flaws.

Welcome to Affirmation Land

Positive affirmations (when you affirm something positive about yourself or your life) are easily one of the best life changing tools out there.

But, if you've ever tried using positive affirmations, you've probably, at least sometimes, felt like a big fat liar. You know, when you try to affirm one thing, but feel or believe another.

(If you're new to the whole *positive affirmation* thing, don't be discouraged by my intro. You'll understand it soon enough!)

On one hand, you're trying to be positive, but on the other hand, you keep reality-checking yourself.

You want to believe what you are saying, but it's too far a stretch or feels just plain fraudulent!

The problem is, people who use positive affirmations do so because they want to feel better. Which means they don't currently feel all that great. And you just can't confidently affirm great things unless you already feel great! It defies the laws of nature.

When you feel like a total failure and try to affirm "I am an amazing success. Everything I touch turns to gold." How do you really feel? Like a liar? A fake? Even more of a failure now because you're not actually an amazing success who turns things to gold?! It's frustrating. And frustration helps no one.

Frustration only creates resistance. Resistance is the exact opposite of what we are going for here. Instead, we want to find a different R-word.

Relief.

That is why this book is different than any other book out there. It's not your typical positive affirmation book that's so overly positive you'll want to puke.

This is a no b.s. self-empowerment book for people who are looking to step into their power and win at life through the successful (key word here) use of affirmations.

I will teach you everything you'll ever need to know to finally make affirmations work for you, once and for all.

If you're new to affirmations, this book will give you one of the greatest tools for creating a life that you love.

Feeling like the victim of your life will be a thing of the past and you'll be the one in control from here on out. Life is gonna start happening *for* you, rather than *to* you and you'll learn how to become the ultimate creator of your own reality.

How's that for a conversation starter?

"WHAT DO YOU DO?"

"OH, I'M JUST THE ULTIMATE CREATOR OF MY OWN REALITY."

If you've already had some experience with positive affirmations, this book will be your new affirmation bible and take you to the next level.

No more corny affirmations to fraudulently repeat over and over until you die. No more feeling like a total failure because affirmations are just reminders that you haven't "made it" yet.

This book not only has tons of affirmations for when you're feeling high on life, but also affirmations for when you're feeling frustrated and need some encouragement.

The affirmations in this book are designed to provide support and relief for you in any moment when you're willing to see things differently (instead of bringing you a sense of discord, like most overly positive affirmations). They will lift you from whatever you're feeling to the next-best mood within reach.

You simply can't affirm super-positive things all the time, but you can always affirm things that feel slightly better. And even slight relief is a step in the right direction.

You'll also learn how to craft your own personal affirmations that will not only help you get clear about what you want, but will also help you create it! You'll learn powerful and exciting formulas for making affirmations work, but most importantly you'll realize just how powerful you truly are.

By the end of this book, you'll be affirming your way to greatness, without feeling like you have to fake it till you make it.

"Actually, I can."

When I first started my inspirational blog (kelseyaida.com), I had no idea if I could actually pull it off. I mean, anyone can start a blog nowadays, but could I really help to create a shift in global consciousness?! I didn't just want to write articles to write articles. I wanted to write articles to change people's lives. I wanted to start a movement, to show people how to tap into their personal power and start winning at life!

But my ego was very quick to remind me of what most people would consider disqualifications. I was only a 22-year-old girl who didn't even go to college. (Ouch) I couldn't be a writer! And I sure as hell didn't know anything about blogging. Clearly, I was in way over my head. Just a silly girl trying to change the world.

Then, as the universe would have it, I stumbled upon a positive affirmation that was going around the internet: **Actually, I can.**

So I changed my inner dialog. Whenever my ego would try to burst my bubble, I would just shut it up with my new affirmation.

You can't be the next Tony Robbins and help millions of people.

Actually, I can.

You can't make a (better than) full time living off a stupid blog.

Actually, I can.

You're practically still a kid; you can't teach people about life.

Actually, I can. (Especially because I have the highest diploma from the "School of Life" to show for it: happiness.)

I even made part of the password that I use to log into my blog "Actually, I can". Every time I start working, I have to type it out and remind myself that actually, I can.

And now I'm really doing it! I'm already reaching thousands of people with my message. People are emailing me every day to tell me how such and such article helped them change their life. I even wrote this book for crying out loud!

So the next time someone (cough cough, your ego) tells you that you can't, now you have the perfect comeback.
#ACTUALLYICAN

affirm

[uh-furm]

(verb)

to state or assert positively;
maintain as true:
*She/He affirmed it the way she
wished it would be until it was so.*

Affirmations are simply things that we say to ourselves either in our heads or out loud. Anytime we affirm something an affirmation is born.

The problem is that we usually affirm the same negative stuff we affirmed yesterday and the day before, because our ego is primarily running the show. If you ask me, this is not only pretty boring, it's also extremely limiting.

SAME THOUGHTS

CHANGE YOUR
CHANGE YOUR

= SAME LIFE

THOUGHTS,
LIFE.

"God's wealth flows to me in avalanches of abundance!"

One day my little sister Bria (short for Sabrina) adopted a new affirmation that she learned from Tony Robbins:

"God's wealth flows to me in avalanches of abundance."

(Apparently he used to recite this affirmation a lot when he was poor, so it obviously worked for him.
#THATSANUNDERSTATEMENT)

She had been feeling pretty poor because we'd just taken lots of (expensive) trips that summer and she'd been in debt to me ever since. Not to mention she was a college student who was transitioning between jobs, which didn't help.

One inspired morning, she wrote her new affirmation in her journal three times.

"God's wealth flows to me in avalanches of abundance.
God's wealth flows to me in avalanches of abundance.
God's wealth flows to me in avalanches of abundance."

Later that day she went on as usual and attended a dance class only to become discouraged when she realized that she didn't even have enough money on her debit card to pay for the class! Luckily her nice friend spotted her and it was no big deal. But after class, all the dancers went out to dinner and again Bria was short on funds. She only had $10 on her debit card, but she was gonna need at least $13 if she wanted to eat anything.

So she desperately checked her purse to see if just maybe there was some leftover cash she may have forgotten about in there. And you know what she found?!

$200 cash. **#TRUESTORY**

A quick rant about your ego

Your ego is that little voice inside your head that you think is you, but actually isn't.

In the days of cave people and saber-tooth tigers, the ego helped to keep us safe, by convincing us to stay in our comfort zones and not do anything too new or dangerous. Today, it just gets in the way of personal growth.

"I'm bad with numbers."

"I never get it right."

"Everyone hates me."

"Life is hard."

"I'm always injured."

Any of these sound familiar?

We do this practically all day, every day, without even realizing it! It wouldn't be such a big deal if our thinking didn't affect our lives much, but it does. In fact, our thoughts are what create our reality.

"SOME PEOPLE SAY THAT AFFIRMATIONS DON'T WORK, WHICH IS AN AFFIRMATION IN ITSELF."

-Louise Hay

Two gigantic, indisputable reasons why affirmations matter (a lot)

Basically, there are two huge reasons why affirmations matter. The first is that using affirmations is a surefire way to reprogram your subconscious mind (which controls your whole life). The second is that affirmations help you leverage the law of attraction (which also controls your whole life). So, either way you slice it, affirmations have the ability to run your life, for better or worse.

The subconscious mind is extremely powerful. If you've ever taken a psychology class you've seen the famous metaphorical picture of your conscious and subconscious mind in the form of an iceberg. The tip of the iceberg (above the water) represents your conscious mind, and the huge base of the iceberg that's hidden under the water's surface represents your subconscious mind.

Not only does it store all your memories and regulate your body temperature, but most importantly, it houses your self-image and works around the clock to make sure your behavior is aligned with your habits, experiences, thoughts, beliefs, hopes, and desires.

It's basically the self-concept police.

If you try to do anything that you haven't done before, your subconscious will be like, "Hey! What do you think you're doing? That's not who you are!" or better yet, "That's not who you *think* you are!" According to your subconscious, everything you say and do must be consistent with your self-concept, or else.

Affirmations are such a great tool because they can be used to alter or improve your self-image. You can craft your true identity and be the best version of yourself.

Unlike the conscious mind, which can easily learn new things, the subconscious mind can only absorb information in three ways. Luckily, habitual repetition (aka practicing affirmations) is one of them.

(In case you're dying of curiosity, the other two ways the subconscious mind can be taught are, according to Bruce H. Lipton, Ph.D., through hypnosis and "super-learning".)

Affirming something once is like a tiny scratch on the surface of your brain. Over time, all the scratches add up to make a deep groove. This means that if you practice an affirmation or thought pattern long enough, it will eventually imprint on your subconscious mind. For better or worse. That's why it is imperative that we choose the thoughts and beliefs that make it to our subconscious. Sift through the good and the bad. Because these beliefs are what inevitably sculpt our self-image and run our lives.

Now that we've covered the standard subconscious reprogramming approach that is taught and accepted by most psychologists, let's dive into a more energy-based explanation as to how affirmations affect our lives, thanks to the law of attraction.

Moving into quantum physics mode. Everything at its most fundamental level is made up of pure energy. The chair you're sitting on is essentially energy. You're energy. I'm energy. Our thoughts are energy. Everything is energetic and therefore has a certain vibration.

The law of attraction is a universal law (similar to the law of gravity in the sense that it produces consistent results) which states that *like energy attracts like energy*. Remember how I said that your thoughts are energy? This means that your thoughts literally attract things (people, experiences, other thoughts) that are like themselves.

This is where the sayings "your vibe attracts your tribe" and "where attention goes, energy flows" come from.

In the most basic explanation, when you think positive thoughts, you attract positive things and experiences into your life and vice versa. It's a direct cause-and-effect relationship.

But our thoughts are not the end-all-be-all of what we attract into our life experience, as is commonly taught. It's actually our mood that the Universe predominantly responds to. Our thoughts are just what affect our mood.

Our mood is the real money-maker. (I mean this figuratively and literally.)

Your mood is a direct indicator of your personal vibration at any given moment. When you feel bad (depressed, angry, jealous, fearful, stressed…) you are vibrating at a low frequency. When you feel good (happy, thankful, loving, excited, hopeful…) you are vibrating at a high frequency.

The law of attraction first and foremost always directly reflects this vibration. So, while yes, you attract what you focus on, more importantly, your thoughts create your feelings and you attract what you feel.

Therefore, your thoughts create your reality, by creating your vibration, which attracts people, places, things, and experiences that match it!

Think about the people you know. Everybody knows that one person who is always feeling shitty and complaining about their life. It feels bad to be around this person and, to put it bluntly, their life sucks.

Seems like bad things are always happening to them. On the outside they look plain unlucky, but really the law of attraction is just doing its job and matching them up with unfortunate events that coincide with their low-frequency vibration.

Their point of attraction is so low that they only match things with a similarly low-frequency vibration! This, in turn, makes them more unhappy, which lowers their point of attraction even more! It can be a vicious cycle if you don't know how to get out.

On the other hand, everybody knows someone who's life seems perfect. They are always smiling and oozing with charisma. Everything they touch turns to gold. Their work life is perfect. Their love life is perfect. They get everything they want.

They are considered the "lucky ones". But this is no accident. These are really the high-vibrational ones, and attract circumstances that reflect their mood and attitude about life.

Everybody wants to be this person, and the use of affirmations is a great way to get there.

Affirmations, or rather *positive* affirmations, are a tool to help you focus on what you want AND get to a good-feeling vibration all at the same time. They're a double-whammy! This is what makes them one of the best tools for using the law of attraction to your advantage.

Killing two birds with one stone

Affirmations play a huge role in the creative process. By *creative* process I mean manifestation. This is how you turn your thoughts into things, and your dreams into reality.

If you'll excuse the morbid expression, affirmations really do kill two birds with one stone when it comes to the creative process.

The creative process basically goes like this: we ask, the universe hears us, and then we receive.

Affirmations can do a lot of the heavy lifting for us because not only are they tools for asking, they also prime us to receive! That's step one and three, which are your only two responsibilities. Done and done! **#THATWASEASY**

[man-uh-fest]

manifest

(verb)

to create an experience in your
life by way of your thoughts,
feeling and emotions:
*They manifested everything on
purpose, with purpose.*

An in-depth look at the creative process

Step one is to ask. This is where you define what you want and then ask for it. How do we ask? Well, we can ask silently in our heads or out loud in the form of a request ("Hey Universe, send me some _____") or an affirmation ("I am _____"), but how we really ask is with our focus!

Whatever we focus on is what we are asking for.

That's why people who only focus on the negative aspects of their life are always getting more "bad luck" and positively focused people always seem so "blessed". They are literally asking for it with their focus.

Practicing positive affirmations is one way to deliberately focus on what we want for long enough that our desires begin to gain some momentum.

In this step, focus wholeheartedly on what you want to bring into your life experience. It can be love, a new job, cool like-minded people… anything! Any thing or experience can be yours. If you can imagine it, the Universe can deliver it. (Heck, even if you can't imagine it, the Universe can still deliver it. It's a true mind-blower sometimes.)

Be careful that when you're focusing on what you want, you're not secretly focused more on the fact that you don't have it yet. You cannot manifest new things if you keep focusing on your present circumstances. Just put the present moment aside and imagine what it will feel like when your wish is already fulfilled (because it will come to life if you let it). The best manifestors are those who can live more in their imagination than in boring, old, reality.

Affirmations can be tricky in this sense, because if when you say them they just remind you that you don't have something or are not yet the person you want to be, then you should not use them. That would be counter-productive. Instead, only use affirmations that make you feel good when you say them.

Let's go back to focusing on what you want more than what you don't want. For example, you want a new car. But every time you think about how you want a new car you are really thinking about how much you hate your current car. So really, you're focused more on your current car.

The door handle is broken, the stupid windows don't even roll up anymore, it gets the worst mileage, the AC is broken… the list goes on. You obviously hate it and are using all these reasons to justify why you need a new car. But where in all of those thoughts is the new car?

Nowhere.

And that's why it's not coming. You think you are focused on a new car when really you are focusing on the current car, the exact thing you are trying to get away from.

An exercise that helps me to focus and deliberately (key word) manifest is to write down affirmations that will be true once I have realized my manifestation in full. "I feel happy. I feel fulfilled. I feel loved. I feel safe. I feel rich…"

Take yourself there with your imagination. This really helps capture the emotion of what you're seeking to manifest and understand the reason behind why you even want it in the first place.

Step two is super-easy because you don't have to do a single thing. This is when the Universe responds to your request. And by respond, I mean it says "yes".

The Universe always, and I mean always, says "yes" to everything you think and feel.

There's an affirmation for ya!

"The Universe says 'yes' to everything I think and feel."

You don't have to do anything here. Just sit back, relax and trust that the Universe is working on your order. Know and expect that your manifestation is on its way. If you can think of it, you can manifest it. The Universe wouldn't plant an idea or inspiration in your head that it could not achieve for you. That would just be plain rude!

When you order food at a restaurant, you don't worry about whether or not they will actually bring it to you. You expect that, because you ordered it, it's coming. It's a done deal. You don't obsess over how they will prepare it or exactly when it will get to your table. You just order something from the menu that sounds yummy and know that it will be delivered to your table just as soon as it has been perfectly prepared. In the mean time, you just enjoy the company of whoever you are with and then the food comes, just as you expected.

You should interact with the Universe in the same way.

Order something from the catalog of life and trust that it is coming. Somehow, someway… Don't worry about how or when, the Universe is very creative and a lot smarter than you.

Once you ask, it is already given. In the meantime, enjoy yourself.

The third and final step is where most people blow it and then get mad because "the law of attraction doesn't work". Step three is to match and receive. You have to match your vibrational frequency to that of what you are asking for and then be in the right space to receive it.

To do this, simply change your thoughts to change your mood (aka use affirmations). Practice, recite and obsess over positive affirmations that make you feel good.

Chances are, you are trying to manifest something that you think is going to make you feel better in some way (aka more high-vibrational). So you have to raise your vibration *before* you can attract your desire into your experience.

Practice affirming how you want your life to be and your life will eventually catch up to your vision.

Everyone is doing it backward!

"When I'm rich, I'll feel abundant."

"When I'm skinny, I'll feel sexy."

"When I get that promotion, I'll be successful."

Instead of creating things on purpose, people are letting their lives happen *to* them, by default. They are constantly just responding and reacting to their pre-existing environment, which is keeping them attached to the same feeling, in the same situations, with the same stuff - forever!

You must find, and hold on to, the new desired feeling first. Then (and only then) can the manifestation occur because like energy attracts like energy. Simply put, your energy has to match that of what you are asking for in order for it to come anywhere near you.

When you feel grateful you will attract more experiences that make you feel grateful.

When you feel frustrated you will attract more experiences that make you feel frustrated.

When you feel abundant you will attract more experiences that make you feel abundant.

Another place affirmations come in handy is when you're ready to be in a space of nonresistance so you can receive or realize your manifestation in full.

If you want to receive, you have to be in your natural state of wellbeing. You must set aside all negative beliefs and just allow yourself to feel good. (For once in your life, allow yourself to just feel good! You are worthy of everything and anything worth having. Stop getting in your own way.)

When you're ready, affirm the things that your highest self already knows to be true.

"I am whole."

"I am happy."

"I am healthy."

In addition to using positive affirmations, there are also other ways to step into a place of nonresistance. Meditation is amazing. Doing fun stuff is great. I can find my place of nonresistance when I'm dancing, doing yoga, or styling hair... Any passion where thought stops, time slows down, and you are in the "flow" will help you get into a state of nonresistance. It's a personal thing. Everyone has that one activity where they just get totally lost (in a good way) doing it.

When you stop thought you are open and connected to the Universe. This is when you can receive.

"WHEN YOU FEEL GOOD YOU WILL INEVITABLY, AS A CONSEQUENCE OF THE LAW OF ATTRACTION, ATTRACT MORE GOOD-FEELING THINGS INTO YOUR LIFE. IT'S THE LAW."

Pssst...

A common misconception is that the affirmations themselves are what create your reality, that you are literally speaking things into existence.

"If I affirm 'I am rich beyond belief!' enough times I will just magically, one day, wake up richer than I could ever imagine."

While it sure does feel like magical wizardry when your affirmations take form in real life, it's not really about *what* you are saying as much as *how* you are feeling when you say it.

I'll say that again. **Affirmations are not really about what you are saying, but how you *feel* when you say them.**

Thanks to the good old law of attraction, the Universe responds first and foremost to your vibration. It doesn't understand words. An affirmation by itself is just a bunch of sounds. But how you feel when you say it is everything!

The whole purpose of using affirmations is to give you the feeling that you want the Universe to pick up on and respond to. They are powerful tools for moving energy and raising your vibration. This is how and why they actually work.

This is the secret.

I WANT _____

BECAUSE IT WI

FEEL _____

LL MAKE ME

Imagine you want more money (Who doesn't?), which means that the feeling you are after is wealthiness. So affirming "I am wealthy" (in a perfect world) is supposed to make you feel wealthy. And the purpose of feeling wealthy is so that you can attract real wealth into your life experience. Feel it first, so you can experience it second.

The problem is, the affirmation is not what's doing all the work. The actual affirmation itself is not changing your life. How you feel when you say the affirmation is what changes your life.

Affirmations are just a tool to help you change your vibration… which changes your life.

Once you understand this, you can see how if you say one thing but feel (vibrate) another, the affirmation doesn't work.

For an affirmation to be successful, it has to get you closer to where you want to be (vibrationally speaking).

If you affirm "I love and appreciate myself because I'm an awesome human being." and you feel good (or at least better than you did before) when you say it, it's a success.

If you affirm the exact same thing, but instead you feel worse because you actually don't love yourself, then that particular affirmation, in that particular moment, is a bust.

[suh k-ses]

a successful affirmation

(noun)

one that either a) gives you
some sense of relief or b) helps
you embody the emotion of
what you want to achieve:

"I am not my depression."

When I was in high school, I had to take this horrible prescription medication. A couple weeks into taking the prescription I became very… mean. My mom actually says that I was a "monster". (Jeeze Mom, tell me how you really feel.) You should know that, up until that point, I had always been a relatively happy, bubbly, and nice human.

At first I was just being mean and cynical, but then I graduated to distancing myself from others. Eventually I stopped liking everything I used to love, and ultimately I became severely depressed.

I was diagnosed with dysthymia depression, which is also known as functional depression. It's a type of chronic depression where the person is super-depressed but still able to function in society. Ya know, go to school, hold a job, normal life stuff. But it's extremely dangerous because most people can't even tell that you are dying on the inside and therefore nobody thinks to help you.

Fast-forward through the three years where I struggled with the illness, broke up with my boyfriend, didn't dance (which for me is equivalent to not breathing), almost killed myself (more than once), and barely made it through high school and beauty school… I was still depressed, but I was sick and tired of being sick and tired.

One day I was wondering how I had gotten to this point.

And then I realized something miraculous.

"Wait a minute… I wasn't always this way… I used to be happy… which means that if I was happy once, I could (maybe) be happy again… which means that I am not this depression… I just have depression!

From this moment on, I will stop identifying myself with my depression and treat it like the illness it is. An illness that I can naturally heal from on my own just like I do from all other sickness.

I am not my depression. I'm just me."

You see, when you suffer from depression, it totally consumes you and, to make matters worse, it feels *very* permanent. But as soon as I remembered that I was me and not my depression, everything changed and I began to heal (without meds).
#WINNING

The simple mindset shift from "I am depressed" to "I am not my depression" literally saved my life.

That's the power of an affirmation.

Your emotions

Understanding and using your emotions is the first step to becoming the creator of your own reality and taking your life back. Pay close attention to this part because this whole book is centered around emotions and using them in harmony with affirmations.

From a law of attraction standpoint, your emotions are like a compass that point you straight toward the fulfillment of your deepest desires, since they tell you how close or far you are from realizing your desires in full and, when used correctly, can point you to where you want to go vibrationally.

Like we've established in previous sections, your vibration is the most important thing because the law of attraction is ALWAYS attracting things to you that match your vibration. It responds directly to your vibration and only to your vibration. Not your words, not your vision boards, not your feng shui.

The meat of your manifesting power is in your ability to vibrate higher, and by vibrate higher I mean feel better. Affirmations help with this, because when you feel good you attract good things. And who doesn't want that?!

But I'm not just talking about feeling good by fluke chance. I'm talking about choosing to feel good; feeling good on purpose so you can deliberately attract awesomeness.

Side note: *This does not mean that you have to be happy all the time or that feeling negative emotions is somehow wrong or bad. Ups and downs are a natural flow of life. And we can't even have good-feeling emotions without the contrast of the "bad" ones, right?*

But wouldn't you prefer to be up more than down? That's what I thought.

THE EMOTIONAL GUIDANCE SCALE BY ABRAHAM HICKS

1. JOY/APPRECIATION/EMPOWERED/FREEDOM/LOVE
2. PASSION
3. ENTHUSIASM/EAGERNESS/HAPPINESS
4. POSITIVE EXPECTATION/BELIEF
5. OPTIMISM
6. HOPEFULNESS
7. CONTENTMENT
8. BOREDOM
9. PESSIMISM
10. FRUSTRATION/IRRITATION/IMPATIENCE
11. OVERWHELMENT
12. DISAPPOINTMENT
13. DOUBT
14. WORRY
15. BLAME
16. DISCOURAGEMENT
17. ANGER
18. REVENGE
19. HATRED/RAGE
20. JEALOUSY
21. INSECURITY/GUILT/UNWORTHINESS
22. FEAR/GRIEF/DEPRESSION/DESPAIR/POWERLESSNESS

THE EMOTIONAL GUIDANCE SCALE BY ABRAHAM HICKS

1. JOY/APPRECIATION/EMPOWERED/FREEDOM/LOVE

2. PASSION

3. ENTHUSIASM/EAGERNESS/HAPPINESS

4. POSITIVE EXPECTATION/BELIEF

5. OPTIMISM

6. HOPEFULNESS

7. CONTENTMENT

8. BOREDOM

9. PESSIMISM

10. FRUSTRATION/IRRITATION/IMPATIENCE

11. OVERWHELMENT

12. DISAPPOINTMENT

13. DOUBT

14. WORRY

15. BLAME

16. DISCOURAGEMENT

17. ANGER

18. REVENGE

19. HATRED/RAGE

20. JEALOUSY

21. INSECURITY/GUILT/UNWORTHINESS

22. FEAR/GRIEF/DEPRESSION/DESPAIR/POWERLESSNESS

The scale

One of my favorite teachers on the law of attraction, Abraham, created this awesome guidance scale of our general human emotions. It has many common emotions listed from high vibration to low vibration (top to bottom) and basically demonstrates how, through baby steps, you can raise your vibration by purposefully moving up the emotional scale one emotion at a time.

(This list is from page 114 of "Ask and It Is Given", by Esther and Jerry Hicks, which I highly recommend for everyone and their mother to read.)

The idea is that you can use this knowledge to your advantage and always reach for a slightly better-feeling emotion, no matter where you are on the scale at any time.

Rung-by-rung you can climb your way up the emotional ladder, thus raising your vibration, and getting closer to everything you ever wanted.

Let's quickly walk through some of the main components of this Emotional Guidance Scale.

Depression obviously feels the worst and is when your vibration has hit an all-time low. When you're in this state you are disallowing your manifestations to happen for you because they do not match this energetic state. But from there you can find slight relief in anger. Anger actually feels a little bit better and is therefore higher up on the scale.

Between boredom and contentment, the scale moves from somewhat neutral or complacent vibrations into the higher vibrational moods.

And of course love, and joy are at the pinnacle. This is when you are most open to, and accepting of, your manifestations.

I don't have to tell you that it can be hard to go from a super-negative emotion to a super-positive one in an instant. If you've ever tried to use positive affirmations that were just too positive, you already know this. This scale explains why: the vibrational gap is simply too big. It's easier to move up the scale one mood at a time and raise your vibration in increments.

You can't just jump from emotion to emotion if they are too far apart on the scale. You have to assess where you are and then reach for something slightly better, but still within reach. The closer the emotion is to your current state the more accessible it is to you in that moment.

When you try to skip from one end of the spectrum to the other too quickly, you'll feel discord and resistance, which are sure to hurt your attracting power.

That's why when you're in a negative state you can't just "think positive" and expect it to work. All you can do is think slightly less-negative until eventually you hit the tipping point and begin to feel better and better.

"REACH FOR A BETTER-FEELING THOUGHT."

-Abraham Hicks

It's a natural process that most of us would do on our own anyway, but knowing how it works can help speed it up.

For example, when you're feeling angry you cannot simply change your thought and skip straight to hopefulness because that is too far out of reach. But you could reach for the feeling of worry, which would feel slightly better. And then once you move through worry you can progress to frustration, another step up from where you were, and so on all the way until you feel great!

This is the premise of the Emotional Guidance Scale. Use it to see how you can feel better. It's like a map to feeling good.

Relief is the operative word here. When you find relief you are releasing resistance. When you release resistance, you feel better. When you feel better, you raise your vibration. And when you raise your vibration good things will come.

Relief is always the first step.

Luckily, there are lots of different ways to find relief, such as by meditating, practicing gratitude, doing something fun, praying, simply changing your focus, or by (oh, I don't know) using affirmations!

The goal is to move yourself up the emotional scale from the lower-vibration emotions toward the higher-vibration emotions. When you move up, you're getting closer to everything you've ever wanted. When you move down the scale, you're moving away from your manifestations.

Now, I know what you're probably thinking: "I have to move my heavy self all the way up this freaking ladder just to get to what I want?! Sounds like a terribly difficult chore."

The truth is, your natural state is to be happy and in a space of love. So really, instead of you doing something to feel better, it's more like your *undoing* stuff that keeps you from *naturally* feeling better.

Believe it or not, it's actually harder to feel bad than it is to feel good. It requires way more effort and energy. It just seems like feeling good is hard because we've been practicing feeling bad for such a long time. But if we weren't always holding ourselves back from feeling good then we would always be connected to the natural flow of wellbeing!

You can see this very clearly in little kids. Unless they are in some sort of physical pain or danger, or feeling hungry, they are always happy little creatures. That's because they are still connected to their natural wellbeing. Society hasn't had enough time to totally f them over yet.

Think of this natural flow of wellbeing like the East Australian Current (E.A.C.) in Finding Nemo. It's happy, fun, natural and makes life easy. It gets you from where you are to where you want to go in a jiffy.

Cutting yourself off from
this flow of wellbeing is like
being a turtle and swimming
all the way across the ocean
outside of the E.A.C.!

**"Bye guys, I'm gonna
take the long way. I'll
catch up with you in
another 50 years!"**

STOP PLAYING LIFE ON HARD MODE.

RIDE THE CURRENT. #RIGHTEOUS

Use affirmations to practice choosing better-feeling thoughts and work your way up the Emotional Guidance Scale.

Let's say you're currently feeling discouraged about how you've been performing at work. So naturally you're a little hard on yourself "I suck at this job," "I can't get anything right," "I wish I was as smart as so-and-so…"

To help yourself out of this mental and emotional state you can reach for slightly better-feeling affirmations like, "I'm ready to let go of my self-doubt and start noticing the things I'm good at," "I do get things right on occasion," "I have my smart moments and I'll make a point to notice them more often."

Then, to feel even better… "I am learning to be better at this job every day," "I'm always looking for and appreciating ways that I perform well," "I choose to work smarter, not harder."

And eventually "I can be great at my job," "I trust in my ability to get things right," "I look forward to being super-smart like so-and-so."

Ultimately, you'll reach a place where you can confidently affirm "You know what, I am great at this job!" "I get everything right," "I'm way smarter than so-and-so."

That's how you use your Emotional Guidance Scale in harmony with positive affirmations. Don't worry; you'll get plenty of practice with this in Part Two. All the affirmations there are designed specifically for this process.

Creating your own badass affirmations

Creating an affirmation is very simple. Basically, you just examine what's not working and then affirm how you would like it to be instead.

Choose something that's not ideal and then change it for the better! Take the negative and flip it into a positive.

You get the idea.

(Hint: Use the templates on the following pages to get started.)

LIFE IS REALLY HARD FOR ME.	LIFE FLOWS EASILY FOR ME.
I SUCK AT MATH.	I'M GREAT AT MATH.
I'M NOT WORTHY OF MY DREAMS.	I AM WORTHY OF MY DREAMS.
THE TIMING OF MY LIFE SUCKS.	I TRUST IN THE DIVINE TIMING OF MY LIFE.
I HATE MYSELF FOR THINKING THAT.	I FORGIVE MYSELF FOR THINKING THAT.

I AM

Two of the most powerful words in the English language. Well, really it's what follows the "I am" that's so important.

Too often we go around in life hating on ourselves -

"I am ugly… I am pathetic… I am a loser,"

- only to draw more of those horrible feelings of insecurity and unworthiness into our lives.

Not to mention, from a law of attraction standpoint, you are literally speaking these things into existence. As soon as you say "I am" *something*, the universe agrees with you and reflects that back to you in your life experience.

You- "I am unworthy of praise."

Universe- "Yes, I agree with you. You are unworthy of praise. Here are some real life experiences that will prove that you are indeed unworthy of praise."

But if you affirm "I am worthy of praise," the universe will still (cough, cough, always) agree with you and respond with the usual.

"Yes, you are worthy of praise. Here are some real life experiences that will prove that you are indeed worthy of praise."

So let's talk ourselves up shall we? There are already enough people out to get us in this world.

If we don't believe in ourselves, who will?

Seems like everyone is raving about the benefits of practicing gratitude nowadays. Better sleep, less stress, more happiness, the list goes on for days.

I probably wouldn't have given in to the hype if it hadn't been for my personal experience with gratitude.

When I was recovering from depression, a friend inspired me to create a gratitude journal. I was feeling ok, but not nearly as excited about life as I wanted to be, so I thought, "Why the hell not?"

After just three weeks of writing in my journal, my life felt and looked completely different! A total 180° flip had occurred in my mentality and reality.

I went from being bored, pessimistic and somewhat hopeless to actually feeling happy about my life! This was a miracle considering I hadn't experienced anything close to happiness in three years.

Practicing gratitude literally had me training my brain to focus on the positive. Every day I would be on the lookout for new things to write about in my journal. Every single morning I would wake up to thoughts of things I was grateful for.

I was finally feeling good thanks to my new outlook on life and, as a direct effect, I started attracting all the right people and experiences. It seemed like life was just flowing effortlessly and that good things were always happening to me whereas before I was basically a character from *A Series of Unfortunate Events*.

I AM THANKFUL FOR

I CHO

One of my New Year's resolutions for 2016 was to become a winner, like a lucky person who wins random stuff.

I had never really won anything by "chance" before (I say "chance" because I don't believe in coincidence.), except once I won a free Snapple. And even then I won that my mom accidentally threw away the cap that said I won. Thanks Mom.

So I just decided that this year I would be a winner.

On January 1st, I was flying home from a business trip (and by "business trip" I mean I was performing on stilts) and had a layover in Las Vegas. If you've ever been to the airport in Las Vegas, you know that there are slot machines in every terminal. Since I had nothing better to do, I decided to try my hand at a little gambling. Besides, this was my first chance to win at something. **#EXCITING**

I put two dollars in a slot machine and I won $33 on my first try! I had never even done this before and I had no idea what the heck I was doing, but I won! A profit of 31 dollars was mine for the taking.

When I got back and told my friends about it they were like, "So you just decided to be a winner and then you won?"

"Yup."

DOSE

IT IS MY DOMINANT INTENT TO...

While you may not feel empowered enough to just choose something for yourself, having an intention is the second best thing. Intending to do, be, or have something is the first step in achieving it. Intention precedes action.

Do you intend to practice more kindness? Notice the little things more often? Feel good on purpose?

Intend it with all your might and soon enough you'll be doin' it! (by which I mean "living out your intention". Get your head out of the gutter!)

I am willing to

Being willing is one of the most admirable qualities in the eyes of the Universe. As soon as you are so little as willing, willing to see thing differently, willing to let go, or willing to dream big, the Universe will support you in that willingness. Soon, that willingness will blossom into intention and then decision and so on.

I can

Maybe you're not exactly where you'd like to be right now, but you sure as hell can be! You can be, do, or have anything you can conjure up in your imagination. Anything!

Not to sound like your mother, but you can do it. I believe in you and this affirmation template will help you believe in yourself too.

I let go of/release

Sometimes, when you're feelin' real shitty, the best thing to do is simply to surrender. Let go of it. At this point, you're too exhausted to try and change your mind or take on anything more. How about subtracting instead?

Release it to relieve it.

F

I forgive

Did you know that forgiveness is one of the fastest, if not the fastest, way to increase alpha brainwave activity?! In plain English, this means that forgiveness is the fast track to increasing creativity, promoting relaxation, heightening problem-solving abilities, enhancing our immune systems, and accessing "super-learning" states.

Do not underestimate this f-word.

When you forgive, you are choosing peace for yourself. Whether you're forgiving a friend, family member, your boss, or yourself, it always sets you up for inner success. Don't forgive others to let them off the hook; forgive them so that *you* can have peace. If you want them to have peace too, then that's great, but don't think you have to just go around letting everyone off the hook. Forgive them and wish them the best. Do it as many times as you need.

What to do when you feel like a fraud

The common teaching around affirmations is to "fake it 'till you make it". While that's all fine and dandy, it doesn't always work…

The Universe always knows when you're lying. That's why you gotta believe it wholeheartedly. You gotta *feel* it into existence, not fake it.

Basically, you have two options if you feel like a liar and your affirmation is slapping you in the face.

1. Make the affirmation feel more authentic (or as I like to call it, "soften" the affirmation)

2. Make yourself believe it by changing your beliefs

1. Luckily, you can easily tweak affirmations to make them feel more authentic to you in any given moment. A little trick I like to use is to soften the statement by changing the wording so it doesn't feel so... out of reach. (All the affirmations in Part Two are designed with this technique. The one's at the very beginning of the chapter are the original affirmations and those later are all softened versions.)

Don't waste your time lying and claiming something you totally oppose because it will only create more resistance (which will take you ten steps backward and zero steps forward). Take baby steps, forward.

If "I am a positive person" is too much, you can change it to "I am willing to be a more positive person." See how that could resonate more with you? Or instead of "I am successful" you could say "I can be successful." "I am stress-free" could become "I choose to be stress-free." And so forth.

"I am willing to...", "I can...", and "I choose..." are a few great softening phrases you can whip out at any time. The point is to keep changing the wording until it feels good as you are saying it. That is key.

2. The other option is to just suck it up and believe what you are saying. This sounds really hard, but is actually quite reasonable.

Since beliefs are just thoughts you have practiced over and over, you can practice thinking different thoughts to change them.

Besides, most of your beliefs aren't even *really* yours. They have been so graciously bestowed upon you by society, the media, your parents, bullies, friends... whoever!

The easiest way to change a belief is to provide supporting evidence for a new one. This is something I learned from my man Tony Robbins (love him). First, **decide what you want the new belief to be and then find enough supporting evidence to prove it true**, making the old belief irrelevant.

When you say an affirmation find the areas of your life where it really is true so you can fully stand behind it.

If the affirmation is "I am thankful for all the wonderful people in my life" think of the people you really are thankful for when you say it. Maybe you're not thankful for every single person you've ever interacted with, but focus on your favorites to really capture and embody the feeling of gratitude.

If you believe "I can't be rich because I come from a poor family/neighborhood/situation", then you would want to change that belief to "I can become rich, despite coming from a poor family/neighborhood/situation."

The easiest way to change your belief would be to find as many rich people (who overcame these circumstances) as it takes for you to believe that you can do it too. Tony Robbins, Oprah Winfrey, Ralph Lauren, Leonardo DiCaprio, J.K. Rowling, Steve Jobs, Nicki Minaj, Howard Schultz...

Who knew?

*(**Side tangent about not believing in yourself**: If you're trying on a positive affirmation and you don't believe that it is true, you need to get your perspective on straight because you can be, do, or have anything you want. Anything! That's a fact.)*

If you believe that your life is lacking abundance and you try to affirm "My life is full of abundance", you can change your belief by looking for evidence of the abundance that is already in your life.

If you're reading this, I can guess that you already have a nice home, plenty of yummy food, a car or two, a smart phone, a computer, a giant TV, a family, a job, lots of nice stuff, experiences and a billion other things to be grateful for. Focus on what you do have and you can't help but to feel abundant!

If you believe that life is hard and you try to affirm "Life flows easily and beautifully for me" just think of all the moments when it was easy and beautiful for you until you can stand behind that statement more confidently.

How about all the times someone held a door open for you? Or when your friends helped you move? Or when you got offered a new job?

See, your life's not so hard after all.

Slightly changing your wording or changing your mind are the two key things most people are missing when affirmations don't perform well for them. Here are some other things to consider if you want to be the best!

Not that it's a competition... but still.

BUT FIRST, EMOTIONS

The ironic thing about using affirmations is this: When you've had one of "those" days and you feel super-shitty is when you're really gonna want to affirm, but this is actually the worst time to do it.

When you feel awful, it's usually because you've experienced some sort of (I don't want to say negativity, so let's just call it "contrast" like Abraham Hicks does) contrast. The beauty of this moment is that when you know what you don't want, you realize what you do want. And as soon as this happens, the first thing you're gonna want to do is make what you do want happen, because you're so sick of experiencing what you don't want.

BUT this is a horrible idea.

Why?

Because you need to find some relief first.

You can (maybe) start with the affirmations at the end of the chapters in Part Two to help in the relief process. But if those don't work, just cool off, put this book down, and come back to it later.

Take a nap. Cry it out. Go for a walk. Sit with that feeling.

Any attempt at totally rewriting your life from an all-time low will not work because you can never manifest anything positive from a place of lack or neediness. If you try, you will fail because **when you think about how you *need* something you are literally affirming that you don't already have it.**

In society today, we never take the time to just let our emotions be. We think feeling bad is bad. We label certain feelings as "negative" emotions. But aside from how they can feel at times, there is nothing negative about them! They are just emotions like the rest of them. And without them, we would be numb and life would be boring.

Their absence would make the "positive" emotions irrelevant because you can't have one without the other.

Contrast is everything.

It's ok to feel shitty.

It's ok to cry.

It's ok to scream into your pillow.

It's ok to feel bad.

Just don't stay there forever.

Feel the feeling. Let it be. Accept it. Listen to it.
And when you're ready to find relief, let go.

Only after honoring your emotions and finding
relief can you dive into some powerful
affirmations.

IT'S

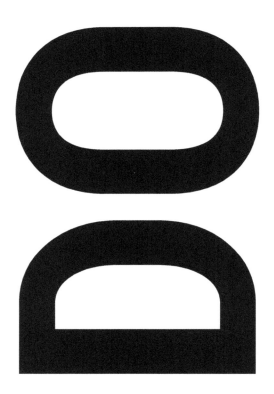

(Always) use present tense

Always affirm things in the present tense as if they were already true. If you affirm that something *will* happen (in the future) it will always stay stuck out there, in the future! No "I will" or "I want" allowed here! All you have is now.

"I am in an unconditionally loving relationship" not "I will be in an unconditionally loving relationship."

Focus on what you want

Always state what you *want*, never what you *don't* want. Whatever you focus on expands.

"My job brings me great satisfaction and sense of purpose" not "My job sucks and is totally unfulfilling."

Try using your name

Affirming things in the third person can sometimes be even more effective than using the first person tense. Especially for people who need a lot of outside reassurance and encouragement. Try pretending you are your favorite school teacher and tell yourself how great you are!

"Kelsey, you are really talented and lovely" instead of "I am really talented and lovely."

DON'T

Forget affirmations are a tool

Although affirmations are game-changing, it's important to remember that they are just one of many tools. Just one more exercise to keep in your self-empowerment back pocket.

Be a hypocrite

If you say your affirmations for one hour every day, but complain the other 23 what do you think will happen? I'll tell you what; a whole lot of nothing!

Make sure your actions match up with your affirmations. Don't just say one thing and then act a different way. That will totally confuse the Universe.

Be the next desperate housewife

Don't try too hard with affirmations. You can feel when you're trying too hard. You have to relax into it, not force it.

If, after the 16th time of saying it, an affirmation gets stale, dump it. If it taunts you when you say it, trash it.

Don't reinforce the fact that what you want hasn't happened yet. If you do, you're actually energetically affirming the opposite of what you're trying to affirm with your words.

WRITE IT & SAY IT

Write them down and say them out loud. Although your thoughts are very powerful, I find that writing down affirmations and then saying them out loud gives them even more power and speed.

Between thinking, writing, speaking, and acting (as in taking inspired action, not faking it) your affirmations are bound to work wonders for you!

"WRITE IT DOWN ON REAL PAPER WITH A REAL PENCIL. AND WATCH SHIT GET REAL."

-Erykah Badu

WARNING: EGO ALERT

Your ego will try to get in your way. It will say things like...
"Who am I to declare myself enough?", "What makes me so
worthy of achieving my dreams?", "I've never been a good
life partner for anybody before why would I be a good one
now just because some blogger says so?", and "I don't deserve
to be blessed as I am." **#WATCHOUTFORTHATEGO**

But eventually, after enough practice, the message you're
trying to adopt will resonate as Truth. Because it is. Deep
down inside, your highest self already knows your Truth. It
always has and it always will. Your Truth is that you are a
perfect, whole, loving, lovable, good, divine, light-filled being.

You just have to go deep enough to tap into that place of
Truth and, BOOM! You will remember who you really are,
and any positive affirmation will feel authentic because it is.

AFFIRM IT O'CLOCK

The most powerful time to use affirmations is when you feel unstoppable. Everybody has those moments where they feel like they are on top of the world and that anything is possible. This is when the best affirmations will actually resonate with you and be most powerful.

Morning (right when you wake up) and night (right before you fall asleep) are super effective times for using affirmations. In the morning, you're setting a positive tone for the day before the day sets the tone for you. At night, you can end the day on a positive note, sleep easy and wake refreshed.

This is not to say that you should ignore the afternoon. On the contrary, the afternoon is the perfect time to reinforce affirmations. Constant reminders throughout the day speed up the process of realizing your affirmation. The more you affirm the something, the quicker it becomes your reality.

Mirror, mirror, on the wall

Use lipstick or (non-permanent) markers to write your affirmations on the bathroom mirror. Heck, write them on all the mirrors!

This is a super fun and effective method because it will be one of the first things you see every morning and every night. Plus you can (and should) recite it out loud while making eye contact with yourself. Reciting affirmations in the mirror is extremely powerful. (Sounds lame, but it works.)

I like to write affirmations on the 70's-style giant wall mirror in my room. It's the first thing I see every day when I get up. As I stand in front of the mirror I read the chosen affirmation of the week with an inspired confidence to start my day off right.

Ding!

Make phone reminders to say (or at least think about) your affirmations throughout your day. The more reminders, the better.

Post that shit everywhere

Use sticky notes to put affirmations all over your life! Place sticky notes in your car, at your desk, in the fridge. Wherever!

Splish splash

If you're embarrassed or shy to get caught reciting affirmations, say them in the privacy of your shower. Recite them over and over until you feel it.

It's also fun to write them on the shower door with your finger. **#JUSTSAYIN**

Ink yourself

Better yet, get a tattoo. Why not?

Your favorite place in the kitchen

This is a fun one if you have kids. Spell the affirmations out on your fridge in magnets. If you don't have magnets, revert back to the sticky note plan.

And there you have it folks! That's about everything you'll ever need to know about affirmations and how to get them to actually work for you. You are officially ready to start affirming yourself to greatness.

Part Two is organized into sections according to the area of your life that you'd like to improve and then further organized according to where you are emotionally. You don't have to read this part in order. Start with whatever area of your life you're most excited about right now. If you're not excited about anything, start with something more general, like life or confidence.

If you're not feeling all that great yet, work your way up from the end of the section toward the beginning.

The affirmations are organized according to the Emotional Guidance Scale (on pages 50-51) but that's not to say they're gonna be exactly the same for everyone.

For me to affirm "I am enough." when I'm sad helps lift me up, but this won't be the case for everybody. So just take what you like and leave what you don't. Move the affirmations around if you wish. The most important thing is that you feel good when you say them.

So what are we waiting for? Let's get to it!

2

PART 2: KICK-ASS AFFIRMATIONS THAT WILL CHANGE EVERY MAJOR ASPECT OF YOUR LIFE FOR THE BETTER

Decoding Part Two

Each section from here on looks something like the following pages. All the affirmations fit under a specific mood category. The mood categories are based directly on the Emotional Guidance Scale by Abraham Hicks and have corresponding hashtags because, frankly, I'm a little obsessed. **#WHATCANISAY**

The categories start at the top of the emotional scale and go down from there. In any given moment, you can pick which hashtag best describes how you're currently feeling and use those affirmations to help lift you to the next mood within reach. It's as easy as that!

The breakdown

When you're feelin' like the bomb.com (#WINNING)

Great for emotions 1-2 **(JOY, APPRECIATION, EMPOWERMENT, FREEDOM, LOVE, PASSION)** on the Emotional Guidance Scale.

These affirmations are for when you are at your peak state and connected to your highest self. When you are in this space, you can pretty much confidently affirm anything. You feel on top of the world and ready to create. These affirmations are some of the strongest, most assertive and powerful.

When you're excited because life is good (#HELLYEAH)

Great for emotions 3-6 **(ENTHUSIASM, EAGERNESS, HAPPINESS, POSITIVE EXPECTATION, BELIEF, OPTIMISM, HOPEFULNESS)** on the Emotional Guidance Scale.

These affirmations are for when you are just within reach of feeling amazing, but not quite there yet. You feel good and are excited or at least hopeful for the future. These affirmations are designed to build confidence and work toward reaching your peak state.

When all you can say is "eh."
(#EH)

Good for emotions 7-8 **(CONTENTMENT/ BOREDOM)** on the Emotional Guidance Scale.

These types of affirmations are meant to guide you up the scale when you are right between feeling good and bad. You're not really happy, but you're not really sad either; you're just sorta ok. Here is where you can take back your power, be assertive, and move in a more positive direction.

When you have ants in your pants and you're slightly PO'd
(#GRR)

Good for emotions 9-10 **(PESSIMISM, FRUSTRATION, IRRITATION, IMPATIENCE)** on the Emotional Guidance Scale.

These affirmations are for softening resistance when you're in a funk. You're pretty fed up and antsy at this point. Here is where you can slow the negative momentum and find some relief before it's too late.

When you feel like you're drowning (#SIGH)

Good for emotions 11-22 **(OVERWHELMENT, DISAPPOINTMENT, DOUBT, WORRY, BLAME, DISCOURAGEMENT, ANGER, REVENGE, HATRED, RAGE, JEALOUSY, INSECURITY, GUILT, UNWORTHINESS, FEAR, GRIEF, DEPRESSION, DESPAIR, POWERLESSNESS)** on the Emotional Guidance Scale.

These affirmations are for softening resistance when you're feeling real shitty. You're done, you've hit rock bottom and you're desperate for a way out. You feel overwhelmed, disappointed, doubtful, and even worried or scared. Here is where you can release some heavy negativity and find relief through surrender.

LOVE Y

Affirmations for radical self-love and unshakable confidence

Loving yourself is the first thing that needs to happen before you can truly love anything or anyone else. It is the whole purpose of why "self-help" even exists and thrives as a market. (For the record, I don't think you need help. I think you have just forgotten how amazing you really are.)

It's astonishing how hard it is for us to love ourselves. But it's not surprising given how life works nowadays. You are born knowing exactly how worthy you are and embracing your divine awesomeness. As you grow, your parents tell you to be "realistic" about your dreams. Then, for 12-16+ years of school, your teachers try to stuff you into a standardized box of littleness. And eventually, the rest of society slowly chips away at your self-worth one sabotaging message and experience at a time. It tells you you're not sexy enough, smart enough, or good enough. But that's not the truth.

The truth is you are everything and more. And these affirmations are here to remind you.

I HAVE UNLIMITED PERSONAL POWER.
I AM BEAUTIFUL INSIDE AND OUT.
**I DON'T GIVE A FUCK ABOUT WHAT ANYBODY
THINKS ABOUT ME BECAUSE THAT IS PART OF
THEIR EXPERIENCE, NOT MINE.**

#WINNING

I AM LOVE.
I AM LIGHT.
I LOVE MYSELF.
BEING ME IS MY
FAVORITE PART OF ALL.
I WAS CREATED PERFECT.
I CAN DO ANYTHING I SET
MY MIND TO.
I RADIATE MY TRUEST
SELF EVERYWHERE I GO.
SELF-LOVING THOUGHTS
COME TO ME
EFFORTLESSLY AND
FREQUENTLY.

I'M A BADASS.
I HONOR WHO I AM BECAUSE I AM
AMAZING.
MY POWER LIES IN MY UNIQUENESS.
I'M MY NUMBER-ONE PRIORITY.
I AM AT PEACE WITH MYSELF.
I GLADLY ACCEPT COMPLIMENTS AND
SUPPORT FROM OTHERS.
I AM UNFUCKWITHABLE.

TODAY, I WILL SEE
MYSELF THROUGH THE
UNCONDITIONALLY
LOVING EYES OF THE
UNIVERSE.
UNLIMITED POTENTIAL IS
WITHIN ME.
**I AM THE CREATOR OF MY
OWN REALITY.**
I OFTEN ASK MYSELF,
"WHAT WOULD SOMEONE
WHO LOVES THEMSELVES
DO?".

I AM THANKFUL FOR MY GIFTS AND
TALENTS.
I VALUE MYSELF.
I BELIEVE IN WHO I AM AND KNOW THAT I
HAVE SO MUCH TO OFFER.
I HAVE AN AMAZING TALENT FOR...

#HELLYEAH

I CARE ABOUT FEELING GOOD.
I CAN LOVE AND ACCEPT MYSELF
BECAUSE I'M AWESOME.
I TRUST THAT I WAS CREATED THIS WAY
FOR A REASON.
I LOOK FORWARD TO EMBRACING
MYSELF BECAUSE IT FEELS GOOD.
I ONLY SEEK TO BE MORE OF MYSELF.

I AM ENOUGH.

You are enough.
You were created enough.
You are more than enough.
You have always been enough.
You are so ridiculously enough it's not even funny.
You are enough to be, do, or have anything that you want.
You are enough.
Period.

#EH

I AM GREAT AT...
I LOVE ... ABOUT MYSELF.
I AM UNASHAMED OF
WHO I AM.
I BELIEVE IN MY ABILITY
TO DO WHAT'S BEST FOR
ME.
I CAN AND I WILL.
I AM PROUD OF MYSELF
FOR...
I TAKE CHARGE OF MY
LIFE.
I ACCEPT MYSELF JUST
THE WAY I AM.
I'M READY TO LOVE
MYSELF.
I CHOOSE LOVING
THOUGHTS OVER
JUDGMENTAL ONES.
**I'LL ONLY LIVE ONCE SO I
MIGHT AS WELL BE A
BADASS. #YOLO**

I MAINTAIN MY CONFIDENCE DESPITE MISTAKES BECAUSE I REALIZE MY MISTAKES ARE OPPORTUNITIES FOR LEARNING.
I CHOOSE TO RESPECT MYSELF TODAY.
I AM LEARNING TO BE MORE SELF-COMPASSIONATE EVERY DAY.
I AM ALWAYS LEARNING NEW WAYS TO APPRECIATE AND LOVE MYSELF.
SELF-LOVE IS MY DIVINE RIGHT AND I'M WILLING TO PRACTICE IT NOW.

MY FALSE PERCEPTIONS OF MYSELF NO LONGER SERVE ME SO I CHOOSE LOVE INSTEAD.
I AM WILLING TO CHANGE MY INNER DIALOGUE ABOUT MYSELF.
WHEN I NEED SOMETHING TO BELIEVE IN I START WITH MYSELF.
I INHALE CONFIDENCE AND EXHALE DOUBT.
I MOVE FORWARD IN SPITE OF MY FEARS.
I DEDICATE MYSELF TO BELIEVING IN MYSELF.

#GRR

I AM ENOUGH.

I AM WILLING TO LET GO OF ANY SELF-DOUBT AND SURRENDER TO SELF-LOVE INSTEAD.

I LET GO OF THE ILLUSION THAT I AM BROKEN AND RECOGNIZE THAT I ALWAYS HAVE, AND ALWAYS WILL BE, WHOLE.

EVERYONE IS ENTITLED TO LOVING THEMSELVES, INCLUDING ME.

#SIGH

I LET GO OF INSECURITIES OF THE PAST.

I CHOOSE TO LIBERATE MYSELF FROM FEELINGS OF DOUBT AND SELF SABOTAGE.

I LET GO OF THE NEED TO BE PERFECT AND EMBRACE MY INDIVIDUALITY.

I FORGIVE MYSELF FOR JUDGING MYSELF.

I LET GO OF ANY NEGATIVE THOUGHTS ABOUT MYSELF AND FOCUS ON WHAT I LIKE ABOUT ME.

ALL YO

Affirmations for kick-ass relationships

Ah… relationships, the very things that hold society together.
We love them and sometimes hate them, but we sure can't live
without them. So why not make the best of them with some
kick-ass affirmations, shall we?

The goal is for all relationships to be centered in a space of
love. Not just romantic love, but all types of love. It feels good
to love your boss, love your family, love your friends and so on.

Use these affirmations to help you get there.

IS L

U NEED

OVE

LOVE IS THE MOST POWERFUL THING OF ALL.

LOVE IS THE ONLY THING THAT'S REAL.

I KEEP MY HEART OPEN AND SHINING.

I LOVE MYSELF AND AM THEREFORE ABLE TO LOVE OTHERS.

#WINNING

MY LOVE IS UNLIMITED.
I AM SURROUNDED BY LOVE.
I RADIATE LOVE.
I AM THANKFUL FOR ALL THE RELATIONSHIPS IN MY LIFE IN ONE WAY OR ANOTHER.
HAPPY AND HEALTHY RELATIONSHIPS COME TO ME EFFORTLESSLY.
I SHOW UP FOR OTHERS.
I AM LOVED.
I AM LOVABLE.

I AM VERY THANKFUL FOR ALL THE WONDERFUL PEOPLE IN MY LIFE.
I FILL MYSELF UP WITH SO MUCH LOVE THAT IT OVERFLOWS ONTO OTHERS.
I FEEL DEEPLY LOVED, RESPECTED, AND APPRECIATED.
LOVE IS AROUND EVERY CORNER.

MY RELATIONSHIPS HELP ME TO BECOME MORE OF WHO I AM.

I FIND JOY WHEN I'M WITH OTHERS.
I ATTRACT LIKE-MINDED PEOPLE INTO
MY LIFE.
I FEEL SUPPORTED BY THE PEOPLE IN MY
LIFE.
IT'S PRETTY EASY TO MAKE COOL
FRIENDS AND ATTRACT NICE PEOPLE
INTO MY LIFE.
I AM READY TO TAKE ON THE WORLD
WITH SOMEBODY AWESOME.
I TRUST AND HONOR MY INTUITION
WHEN IT COMES TO MY RELATIONSHIPS
AND ENCOUNTERS WITH OTHERS.

I CAN BE A GOOD
PARTNER/SIBLING/BOSS.
I TRUST THE DIVINE
TIMING OF THE
RELATIONSHIPS IN MY
LIFE.
I KNOW THAT EVERY
RELATIONSHIP IS AN
OPPORTUNITY TO PROVE
WHO I REALLY AM.
**I CHOOSE TO LOVE
UNCONDITIONALLY.**
RELATIONSHIPS ARE FUN
AND FULFILLING.
I GIVE THE LOVE I WANT.

#HELLYEAH

MY PARTNER MAKES ME FEEL LOVED,
CHERISHED, AND APPRECIATED.
**I LOOK FORWARD TO SPENDING TIME WITH
AWESOME PEOPLE BECAUSE IT FEELS GOOD.**
THE PERFECT PARTNER/EMPLOYER/
FRIEND IS LOOKING FOR ME JUST AS I AM
LOOKING FOR THEM. THE UNIVERSE IS
BRINGING US TOGETHER NOW.
I DON'T NEED ANYONE TO FEEL WHOLE
AND COMPLETE.

LOVE CREATED ME LIKE ITSELF.

Holiness created you holy.
Kindness created you kind.
Helpfulness created you helpful.
Perfection created you perfect.

(excerpt from *A Course In Miracles*)

#EH

I CHOOSE TO LOVE MORE.
I CHOOSE TO SEE PEOPLE
THROUGH THE
UNCONDITIONALLY
LOVING EYES OF THE
UNIVERSE.
I CHOOSE FORGIVENESS
OVER HATRED.
**EVERYBODY COMES INTO MY
LIFE FOR A REASON.**
LIFE IS TOO SHORT TO BE
MAD AT OTHERS.
THE MORE I FORGIVE
MYSELF, THE EASIER IT IS
TO FORGIVE OTHERS.
I AM READY TO FORGIVE
THOSE WHO HAVE
WRONGED ME IN THE
PAST SO I CAN MOVE ON
WITH MY LIFE.
I'M RAISING MY
STANDARDS SO THE
UNIVERSE CAN MEET ME
THERE.

I FORGIVE THOSE WHO HAVE HARMED ME IN THE PAST AND CHOOSE PEACE INSTEAD.
I LET GO OF ALL TOXIC PEOPLE AND SEND THEM OFF WITH LOVE.
I AM LEARNING TO BE MORE FORGIVING EVERY DAY.

#GRR

I AM ALWAYS LEARNING NEW WAYS TO IMPROVE MY RELATIONSHIPS.
A LOVING AND SUPPORTIVE PARTNER/LOVER IS MY DIVINE RIGHT AND I AM OPEN TO MEETING THEM NOW.
I PRACTICE FORGIVENESS FOR MY OWN INNER PEACE.

I RELEASE THE DESPERATE NEED FOR
LOVE AND VALIDATION, AND INSTEAD
GIFT IT TO MYSELF.
I LET GO OF THE FEAR SURROUNDING
THIS RELATIONSHIP AND CHOOSE LOVE
INSTEAD.
I AM SAFE TO BE MYSELF IN MY
RELATIONSHIPS.

#SIGH

I SURRENDER TO LOVE.
I GIVE MYSELF THE GIFT OF SELF-LOVE.
**EVERYONE DESERVES TO BE LOVED,
INCLUDING ME. I ACCEPT LOVE NOW.**
I FORGIVE MYSELF FOR SCREWING UP IN
MY PAST RELATIONSHIPS; I'M ONLY
HUMAN.

HAPPY

HEALTH

WELL -

Affirmations for vibrant health and wellbeing

The first step to a happy, healthy, and well-thy (See what I did there?) life is to embrace a healthy and loving mentality about your body. Your body is your vessel and home. It's imperative to treat it with kindness, gratitude, and respect. **When you love your body your body will love you right back.**

The body and mind are directly connected. All disease first begins in the mind before it manifests in the body. Even if you can't consciously make the connection, it's there. Dis-ease is just the manifestation of wrong thoughts that stem from fear. (Not that you thought wrong on purpose, but it happens.) Therefore, you can rid yourself of disease with right thought; thoughts that stem from love.

Your natural bodily state is one of health and wellbeing. Your body knows how to heal itself, you just have to let it. Have a little faith and choose hope over fear. Vitality will soon be yours for the win!

I LOVE AND TRUST EVERY CELL OF MY BODY.
I'M ALWAYS WELL.
I RADIATE HEALTH AND VITALITY.
HEALTH COMES TO ME NATURALLY AND EFFORTLESSLY.

#WINNING

I AM HAPPY, HEALTHY, AND WHOLE.
I AM THANKFUL FOR EVERY PULSE AND EVERY BREATH.
I FEEL ALIVE, RADIANT, AND WELL.
I'M IN PERFECT HEALTH.
I'M THANKFUL FOR MY HEALTHY BODY.
I LOVE BEING ALIVE.
I LOVE TAKING AMAZING CARE OF MYSELF.
BEING HEALTHY IS ONE OF THE BEST FEELINGS EVER.

I CAN BE HEALTHY.

**I TRUST IN THE DIVINE
INTELLIGENCE OF MY BODY
TO ALWAYS HEAL ITSELF.**

I LOOK FORWARD TO
BEING MORE HEALTHY
BECAUSE IT FEELS GOOD.

HEALTH IS MY NATURAL STATE OF
WELLBEING.
MY BODY IS MY HOME AND I TREAT IT
WITH THE UPMOST RESPECT.
I LOVE MY BODY FOR ALLOWING ME TO
EXPRESS MYSELF THROUGH...

#HELLYEAH

I AM THANKFUL FOR MY BODY'S ABILITY
TO HEAL ITSELF.
I ENJOY TAKING GOOD CARE OF MYSELF.
I TAKE TIME TO NOURISH AND
STRENGTHEN MY BODY.

I TRUST IN THE DIVINE INTELLIGENCE OF MY BODY.

When you get a cut, do you ever wonder if it's gonna get better or do you just expect that it will like it always does? **#TRUSTYOURBODY**

#EH

I CHOOSE TO BE HEALTHY.
I CHOOSE TO MAKE MORE
HEALTHFUL DECISIONS.
I CHOOSE HEALTH OVER
DISEASE.
EVERY DAY I BECOME
MORE AND MORE
RELAXED.
TODAY, I CHOOSE TO BE
RELAXED AND AT EASE
BECAUSE THAT IS WHEN I
FEEL BEST.
**MY BREATH BRINGS ME
PEACE AND HEALING.**
I APPROACH THOUGHTS
ABOUT MY BODY WITH
HOPE RATHER THAN
FEAR.
I AM READY TO THINK
HEALTHY THOUGHTS
AND STOP OBSESSING
OVER EVERY LITTLE ACHE
AND PAIN.
**I'M WRITING A NEW STORY
THAT LOOKS WAY BETTER
THAN MY PAST.**

HEALTH HAPPENS NATURALLY. I LET GO OF THE DESPERATE NEED FOR PERFECT HEALTH AND ALLOW IT TO OCCUR NATURALLY, AS IT WILL. I LET GO OF FOCUSING ON ANY AILMENTS AND INSTEAD FIND GRATITUDE FOR ALL THAT MY BODY DOES FOR ME. I BREATHE IN HEALTH AND EXHALE STRESS. WELLBEING IS EVERYONE'S DIVINE RIGHT, INCLUDING MINE. I AM OPEN TO RECEIVING IT NOW.

MY BODY HAS ALWAYS HEALED ITSELF IN THE PAST AND WILL CONTINUE TO DO SO BECAUSE THAT'S JUST WHAT IT DOES.

#GRR

I GET OUT OF MY OWN WAY AND LET MY
BODY HEAL ITSELF WITH ITS BRILLIANT
INTELLIGENCE.
I LET GO OF ANY TRAPPED EMOTIONS
AND CREATE SPACE FOR LOVE INSTEAD.
I AM NOT MY BODY. I AM AN ETERNAL BEING.

#SIGH

I RELEASE ALL DIS-EASE FROM MY BODY
AND WELCOME VITALITY, HEALTH, AND
RADIANCE NOW.
I GIVE MYSELF PERMISSION TO HEAL.
I LET GO AND TRUST THE HEALING
PROCESS.
MY BODY ALWAYS HEALS ITSELF. IT
KNOWS EXACTLY WHAT TO DO. I DON'T
HAVE TO WORRY ABOUT IT ANYMORE.

SHO

Affirmations for Financial Freedom

Let's face it. We would all like to have more money. Bu
what we're really craving is the feeling of abundance
Never having to stress or worry about finances. Having
the freedom to do what we want, when we want

Like all things in life, our thoughts and feelings abou
money are what create our real-life experience of it. To
create more, we must adopt a mentality of abundance
(not just in finances, but in all aspects of our lives)

These affirmations were created just for that. Use
them, feel them, embrace them and the Universe wil
have no choice but to show you the money

THE M

V ME

ONEY

I AM DESERVING OF AND THANKFUL FOR ALL THE ABUNDANCE THAT COMES MY WAY.
I ENJOY SPENDING MY MONEY ON THINGS THAT MAKE ME FEEL GOOD.
I REALIZE THE VALUE I PROVIDE AND CONFIDENTLY ACCEPT GENEROUS COMPENSATIONS.

#WINNING

MONEY FLOWS EFFORTLESSLY INTO MY LIFE.
EVERY DOLLAR I SPEND COMES BACK TO ME IN DIVIDENDS.
I NEVER HAVE TO WORRY ABOUT MONEY BECAUSE I ALWAYS HAVE MORE THAN ENOUGH.
I FIND SUCCESS WAITING AROUND EVERY CORNER.

I AM THANKFUL FOR WHAT I HAVE AND WELCOME ALL THE GIFTS LIFE WILL BRING.
I AM GREAT WITH MONEY.
I VALUE MYSELF AND MY WORK.
I PAY MY BILLS WITH GRATITUDE FOR THE ABILITY TO DO SO.
HAVING MORE MONEY ALLOWS ME TO BE MORE OF WHO I AM.

EVERY TIME I TURN AROUND, THERE'S A CHECK IN THE MAIL. **I ENJOY HAVING MORE SO I CAN GIVE MORE.** IT FEELS GOOD TO SPEND MONEY BECAUSE I KNOW THERE IS MORE WHERE THAT CAME FROM. I SEE ALL OF THE GOOD THAT WILL COME FROM MY FINANCIAL FREEDOM. IT EXCITES ME TO THINK OF ALL THE GREAT THINGS I CAN DO WITH MY ABUNDANCE.

MY POSITIVE ATTITUDE ALLOWS PROSPERITY TO FLOW INTO MY LIFE. **I AM GOOD ENOUGH TO ACHIEVE MY DREAMS.** I HAVE FAITH IN MY ABILITIES TO ACCUMULATE WEALTH. I TAP INTO MY RECEPTIVE MODE AND RECEIVE ABUNDANCE WITH GRACE AND GRATITUDE.

#HELLYEAH

THE PERFECT MONEY-MAKING OPPORTUNITY IS LOOKING FOR ME JUST LIKE I AM LOOKING FOR IT. THE UNIVERSE IS BRINGING US TOGETHER RIGHT NOW. I LOOK FORWARD TO HAVING MORE MONEY BECAUSE THE MORE I HAVE, THE MORE I CAN GIVE. I TRUST IN MY ABILITY TO CREATE WEALTH FOR MYSELF AND MY FAMILY. I CAN DO THIS, AND I LOOK TO OTHERS WHO ALREADY HAVE DONE THIS FOR INSPIRATION AND GUIDANCE.

ABUNDANCE IS MY BIRTHRIGHT.

Did you know that life is supposed to be abundant?

Did you know that it's ok to want to have things that make your life awesome? (Because the more you have, the more you can give.)

Now the only question left is…

Do you feel that you are worthy?

#EH

I ACCEPT CONFIDENCE
AND COURAGE ON MY
FINANCIAL JOURNEY.
I EMBRACE A LIFE OF
TRUE ABUNDANCE
STARTING NOW.
I AM COMPLETELY ABLE
TO MAKE MONEY.
I ACCEPT A DESTINY OF
ABUNDANCE AND
FREEDOM.
**I AM READY TO START
LIVING AN ABUNDANT LIFE
BY FIRST PRACTICING AN
ABUNDANT MINDSET.**
I CHOOSE TO TRY
SOMETHING NEW
INSTEAD OF GIVING UP.

I ALLOW GUILT TO SLIP AWAY AND REALIZE THAT HAVING MONEY IS SOMETHING TO BE PROUD OF.
I LET GO OF MY *LACK* MENTALITY AND CHOOSE ABUNDANCE INSTEAD.
TODAY, I CHOOSE TO SEE THE GLASS AS HALF FULL INSTEAD OF HALF EMPTY.
I REALIZE THAT THE MORE I APPRECIATE THE MORE I WILL ATTRACT TO BE APPRECIATIVE OF.

ABUNDANCE IS MY DIVINE RIGHT AND I AM OPEN TO CREATING IT NOW.
I AM ALWAYS LEARNING NEW WAYS TO IMPROVE MY FINANCES.
I EDUCATE MYSELF AROUND THE SUBJECT OF WEALTH ACCUMULATION AND MONEY MANAGEMENT.

#GRR

EVERYONE DESERVES TO EXPERIENCE
THE FREEDOM OF WEALTH, INCLUDING
ME.
I AM AT PEACE WITH MY PAST DECISIONS
AND APPRECIATE WHAT I HAVE LEARNED
FROM THEM.
I DESERVE TO HAVE ALL THE GOOD
THINGS THAT COME MY WAY.

#SIGH

I LET GO OF ANY NEGATIVE IDEAS ABOUT
WEALTH AND WEALTHY PEOPLE.

**I LET GO OF MY DESPERATE NEED FOR MONEY
AND INSTEAD GIVE THANKS FOR THE THINGS
MONEY CAN'T BUY.**

I'M DITCHING MY *LACK* MENTALITY AND
ADOPTING AN ABUNDANT MINDSET.
I LET GO OF MY ATTACHMENT TO
MATERIAL THINGS.

DON'T BE RU

HAVE

GRATI

Affirmations for Cultivating Gratitude

Gratitude is one of the most powerful tools for cultivating happiness. Not only does a consistent gratitude practice train your brain to look for the positive things in life, it literally raises your energetic frequency.

Gratitude has been proven to reduce stress, enhance empathy, and improve psychological and physical health. In a 2012 study published in *Personality and Individual Differences*, practicing gratitude even led to fewer doctor visits! In my personal experience, practicing gratitude helps with sleeping well, feeling better, and changing your perspective on life.

After using these affirmations, your perception will be more skewed towards positivity and your mind will constantly look for new things to give thanks about. Plus, every time you appreciate life you are giving it permission to send you more things to be thankful for! It's a beautiful cycle: the more you appreciate, the more you are given to appreciate and so on.

I'M THANKFUL FOR ALL THINGS BIG AND
SMALL.
I'M THANKFUL FOR BLESSINGS AND
CHALLENGES ALIKE BECAUSE BOTH
SERVE MY GROWTH AND EVOLUTION.
I FREAKIN' LOVE MY LIFE!

#WINNING

I AM SERIOUSLY
BLESSED.
I RADIATE GRATITUDE.
BEING GRATEFUL COMES
TO ME EFFORTLESSLY.
**I LOVE MY LIFE LIKE A LITTLE
KID LOVES CHOCOLATE.**
I AM THANKFUL FOR...

CULTIVATING GRATITUDE IS ONE OF THE
BEST FEELINGS EVER.
I LOVE IT WHEN I FEEL GOOD.
I AM OBSESSIVELY GRATEFUL.

I CAN BE GRATEFUL FOR LOTS OF THINGS IN MY LIFE.

I LOVE IT WHEN THINGS WORK OUT IN MY BEST INTEREST WITHOUT ME EVEN REALIZING IT UNTIL LATER.

I'M HAPPY THAT I'M LEARNING HOW TO STEP INTO MY OWN POWER AND WIN AT LIFE.

I KNOW THAT LIFE HAPPENS *FOR* ME, NOT *TO* ME.

I LOOK FORWARD TO RECEIVING EVEN MORE AWESOME BLESSINGS IN MY LIFE. I KNOW THAT BY BEING THANKFUL, I'M ATTRACTING MORE THINGS TO BE THANKFUL FOR.

#HELLYEAH

I'M SAYING "YES!" TO MY LIFE.

I FREAKIN' LOVE HAPPINESS!

#EH

I CHOOSE TO BE
THANKFUL RATHER
THAN NEEDY.
I AM READY TO PRACTICE
MORE GRATITUDE IN MY
LIFE.
**I'M ACTUALLY THANKFUL
THAT I DON'T HAVE
EVERYTHING I EVER WANTED
BECAUSE IF I DID, I WOULD
BE BORED OUT OF MY MIND
WITH NOTHING TO DO OR
WORK TOWARD.**
I'M GRATEFUL THAT I'M
TAKING TIME TO WORK
ON MYSELF.
I CHOOSE TO APPRECIATE
ALL THAT MY LIFE HAS
TO OFFER.

I AM THANKFUL THAT I DON'T HAVE IT ALL.

If this Christmas, Santa offered to give you every single present you would ever get for the rest of your life, would you happily accept the offer?

Didn't think so.

I CAN BE A LITTLE MORE GRATEFUL TODAY. GRATITUDE IS A LEARNED SKILL THAT ANYONE CAN GET GOOD AT, INCLUDING ME.

I AM LEARNING TO BE MORE THANKFUL EVERY SINGLE DAY. I AM ALWAYS LEARNING NEW WAYS TO CULTIVATE GRATITUDE.

#GRR

GRATITUDE HAPPENS NATURALLY. IF I JUST STOP BLOCKING MYSELF OFF FROM IT, IT WILL GROW.

I LET GO OF MY *LACK* MENTALITY AND CHOOSE TO FOCUS ON WHAT GOOD THINGS I DO HAVE.

I FORGIVE MYSELF FOR NOT ALWAYS BEING GRATEFUL; I'M ONLY HUMAN.

I'M THANKFUL FOR THE CONTRAST IN MY LIFE BECAUSE IT HELPS ME TO GET CLEAR ABOUT WHAT I REALLY WANT.

#SIGH

I'M OVER FEELING SO ENTITLED AND CHOOSE TO BE THANKFUL STARTING NOW.

I DESERVE BLESSINGS AND I AM OPEN TO ACCEPTING THEM NOW.

I'M GRATEFUL JUST TO BE ALIVE.

Affirmations for inner peace and stress-free living

Stress. It's a real killer. It kills your dreams, it kills your vibes, and it can even kill you (literally)! But you can never rid yourself of something by focusing or hating on it. So these affirmations are designed to help you ditch stress and replace it with ease instead.

Life is too short to feel so stressed all the time. And life is definitely too short to constantly live in a low-vibrational place of fear, which is what all stress originates from.

It's time to stop wasting precious energy and start redirecting it in a more positive direction.

BYE STRESS

HELLO

EASE

I AM ALWAYS CONNECTED TO MY
HIGHEST SELF.
LIFE FEELS EASIER THAN EVER.
**THE UNIVERSE HAS MY BACK SO I NEVER
NEED TO WORRY.**

#WINNING

I AM PEACE.
I RADIATE CALM.
I FEEL TOTALLY AND
COMPLETELY AT EASE.
I FULLY ACCEPT EVERY
MOMENT.
BEING PRESENT BRINGS
ME PEACE.

I HAVE AN INFINITE NUMBER OF
OPPORTUNITIES AND CHOICES. I NEVER
WORRY ABOUT THINGS NOT WORKING
OUT.
I LIVE IN HARMONY WITH THE UNIVERSE
AND LIFE FLOWS EASILY FOR ME.
EACH DAY LIFE IS FUN, FLOWING AND
NEW.
I AM GRATEFUL FOR EASE AND GRACE.

I TRUST THAT
EVERYTHING IS ALWAYS
WORKING OUT FOR ME.
I EXPECT MIRACLES.
I AM THANKFUL FOR ALL
THE GOOD IN MY LIFE.
I KNOW THE UNIVERSE
KNOWS WHATS BEST
FOR ME.

I CAN BE PEACEFUL.
I KNOW THAT PEACE IS MY NATURAL
STATE OF WELLBEING.
**I LOOK FORWARD TO EMBRACING A STRESS-
FREE LIFESTYLE BECAUSE IT FEELS GOOD TO
ME.**

#HELLYEAH

I'M ABLE TO CALM MYSELF DOWN.
BYE BYE STRESS. HELLO EASE.
DEAR STRESS, I'M DIVORCING YOU.
#SORRYNOTSORRY

CHOOSE PEACE INSTEAD OF THIS.

The absolute fastest way to cut the crap and feel better.

#EH

I CHOOSE TO PRACTICE
PEACE TODAY.
I BELIEVE IN MIRACLES.
I CHOOSE THE TYPE OF
LIFE I WANT TO LIVE AND
I WILL START LIVING IT
NOW.
I DESERVE THE BEST AND
CLAIM IT NOW.
**AT THIS VERY MOMENT,
BLESSINGS ARE AVAILABLE
TO ME AND I CHOOSE TO
EMBRACE THEM WITH
GRATITUDE AND HUMILITY.**
I'M GETTING BETTER AT
SEEING THE POSITIVE IN
EVERY SITUATION.
I'M READY TO EMBRACE
THE LITTLE MOMENTS OF
BLISS AND STOP
WORRYING SO MUCH.
**LIFE WORKS BETTER WHEN I
ENJOY IT.**
THE UNIVERSE HAS MY
BACK. I CAN CHILL.
LIFE IS TOO SHORT TO BE
STRESSED OUT ALL THE
TIME.

PEACE HAPPENS NATURALLY. I LET GO OF THE DESPERATE NEED TO RID MYSELF OF STRESS AND INSTEAD ALLOW PEACE AND CALM TO OCCUR NATURALLY.
FROM NOW ON I'LL STOP PLAYING LIFE ON HARD MODE AND CHOOSE TO GO WITH THE FLOW.
I RELEASE ALL LITTLENESS AND CHOOSE GREATNESS INSTEAD.
WHEN I COME FROM A PLACE OF LOVE, I CAN CREATE MY LIFE WITH STYLE AND EASE.

I GET TO CHOOSE HOW I FEEL.
I AM LEARNING TO BE MORE CENTERED EVERY DAY.
PEACE IS MY DIVINE RIGHT AND I AM OPEN TO ACCEPTING IT NOW.
I CAN WAIT.

#GRR

I LET GO OF STRESS BECAUSE IT DOES
NOT SERVE ME.
I GIVE MYSELF THE GIFT OF SURRENDER.
I'M LEAVING MY STRESS WITH THE
UNIVERSE AND CALLING IT A DAY.
I AM WILLING TO SEE THINGS DIFFERENTLY.
I RELEASE ALL JUDGEMENT AND ACCEPT
THE "ISNESS" OF ALL SITUATIONS.
NOTHING IS GOOD OR BAD UNTIL I LABEL
IT AS SUCH.
I COULD FOCUS ON MY BREATHING.

#SIGH

I LET GO OF FEAR AND CHOOSE LOVE
INSTEAD.
I AM NOW WILLING TO BE OPEN TO ALL
THAT LIFE HAS TO OFFER.
**I LET GO OF STRUGGLE AND SURRENDER TO
EASE.**
I GET TO CHOOSE WHO I AM.
I INTERRUPT ANXIETY WITH GRATITUDE.
I QUIT PLAYING LIFE ON HARD MODE AND
RIDE THE CURRENT.
PEACE COMES NATURALLY WHEN I STOP
RESISTING IT.

Fly grasshopper

Consider this book your new best friend. Like a good friend, it's here for you whenever you need it. You can cry on its shoulder, laugh with it, feel good and be yourself around it.

Reference it often for inspiration and empowerment. Use the crap out of it to feel better and start winning at life.

With these affirmations in play, be prepared for some radically positive change. Don't be surprised when your life starts to look as good on the outside as it now feels on the inside. Because it's already happening.

Get excited for what your future holds because it's shining real bright now! Just like you.

And with all that being said, I leave you with one more affirmation from me to you.

#ACTUALLYYOUCAN

Love and Light,
Kelsey Aida

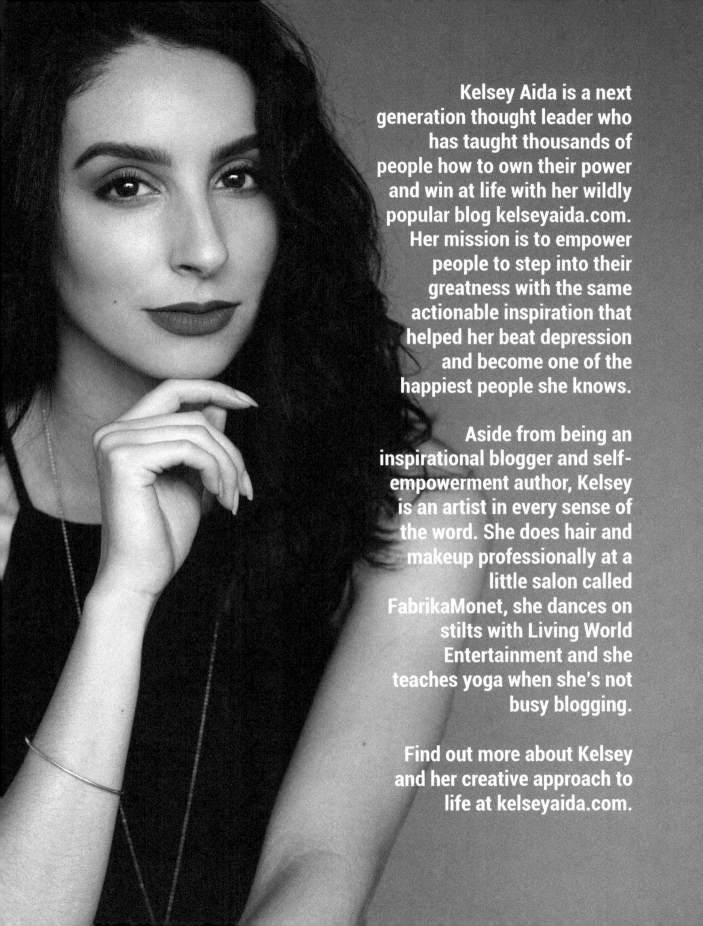

Kelsey Aida is a next generation thought leader who has taught thousands of people how to own their power and win at life with her wildly popular blog kelseyaida.com. Her mission is to empower people to step into their greatness with the same actionable inspiration that helped her beat depression and become one of the happiest people she knows.

Aside from being an inspirational blogger and self-empowerment author, Kelsey is an artist in every sense of the word. She does hair and makeup professionally at a little salon called FabrikaMonet, she dances on stilts with Living World Entertainment and she teaches yoga when she's not busy blogging.

Find out more about Kelsey and her creative approach to life at kelseyaida.com.

Lightning Source UK Ltd.
Milton Keynes UK
UKHW05f0858140818
327177UK00028B/1725/P